Military Dune Buggies

by Michael Green

Reading Consultant:
Sergeant James Petersen (retired)
United States Air Force

C A P S T O N E   P R E S S
M A N K A T O ,   M I N N E S O T A

C A P S T O N E   P R E S S
818 North Willow Street • Mankato, Minnesota 56001

Library of Congress Cataloging-in-Publication Data
Green, Michael, 1952–
   Military dune buggies/by Michael Green.
   p. cm. — (Land and sea (Mankato, Minn.))
   Includes bibliographical references and index.
   Summary: Discusses the history and use of military dune buggies, highlighting specific models and their roles in various battles.
   ISBN 1-56065-461-9
   1. Desert patrol vehicle—Juvenile literature. [1. Desert patrol vehicle.]
I. Title. II. Series.
UG615.G74 1997
623.7'472—dc21

                                        96-44343
                                           CIP
                                            AC

Photo credits
Chenowth: 4, 6, 20, 24, 28-33
Michael Green:10
Patton Museum: 8, 12, 14
U.S. Army: 16, 22, 34-47
U.S. Navy: 26

Table of Contents

Features

Pronunciation guides follow difficult words, both in the text and in the Words to Know section in the back of the book.

Chapter 1

Military Dune Buggies

Every army has scouts, and every army has scout vehicles. Scouts are people who spy on enemy troops. Scouts are the eyes and ears of an army. Scout vehicles are the machines scouts drive while they are spying. Military dune buggies are scout vehicles.

Scout vehicles are normally very small. They can be hidden easily from the enemy. They are armed with light weaponry so scouts can defend themselves if they are spotted.

Military dune buggies are used as scout vehicles.

Perfect Scouts

Dune buggies make perfect scout vehicles.
They are built out of metal tubing. They have
four tires. Dune buggies are powered by
Volkswagen engines. Volkswagen is a German
carmaker. The Volkswagen engines in dune
buggies are cheap to build and easy to fix.

Dune buggies have not always been military
scout vehicles. Dune buggies first appeared in
Southern California in the early 1960s. They

Dune buggies are great off-road military vehicles.

were built in garages and backyards by fans of off-road driving.

Off-road fans wanted a lightweight vehicle that could travel across sand dunes. They wanted a vehicle that could be used for fun. They never thought their dune buggies would become military scout vehicles.

Chapter 2

Early Scout Vehicles

In early military history, scouts moved around on their feet or on horses. But the development of the gasoline engine changed things.

The gasoline engine allowed armies to give their scouts motorized transportation. In the 1930s, the U.S. Army gave its scouts motorcycles. By 1941, the army gave its scouts the M20 armored car. Armor is anything used to protect vehicles, people, and cargo during combat. Armor is usually steel.

Military scouts used to ride horses.

The M20

The M20's thin armor offered little protection from most enemy weapons. It was armed with a single machine gun. Its best defense was to avoid being seen by the enemy.

The M20 had six wheels and was powered by a gasoline engine. Its top speed was 55 miles (88 kilometers) per hour. At the time, it was the fastest armored car in the world.

The M20 performed well under most conditions. But enemy soldiers found that it was

The M20 was used by the U.S. Army during World War II.

easy to throw hand grenades into the vehicle.
And on muddy ground, the M20 often got stuck.
A stuck scout vehicle can be spotted easily by
the enemy.

Scouts on Tanks

So the army had its scouts ride on tanks. Tanks
are enclosed vehicles protected with heavy
armor. Tanks are mounted with various weapons,
one of which is usually a large cannon.

For extra traction, tanks move on tracks. Tracks are metal belts that run around wheels on both sides of a vehicle. Tanks could cross muddy ground without as much trouble as the M20. But tanks were a problem for scouts because they were very noisy.

U.S. soldiers wanted a vehicle that was quieter than the tanks. They wanted a vehicle that was not as easy to target as the M20.

Tracked Scout Vehicle

The M20 was replaced in the early 1960s by an armored vehicle known as the M114. The

The M114 replaced the M20.

M114 was about 14 feet (five meters) long and seven feet (two meters) tall.

A commander, a driver, and a radio operator made up the M114's crew of three. Early models were armed with two machine guns. Later models were armed with a 20 millimeter (mm) cannon. The millimeters measure the diameter of the cannon's barrel.

Midway

Midway is an island in the Pacific Ocean. The battle of Midway was fought June 3-6, 1942, during World War II.

U.S. scout planes spotted Japanese ships and radioed the information back to U.S. aircraft carriers. Bombers and torpedo planes on the carriers used the information from the scouts to destroy much of the Japanese navy.

The battle of Midway was a major victory for U.S. forces, thanks to the scouts.

The M114 had an armored aluminum hull. The hull is the main body. The gasoline engine was in the front of the vehicle. The M114's top speed was 36 miles (58 kilometers) per hour. It could go 300 miles (480 kilometers) on a full load of fuel.

The M114 was not a success for the U.S. Army.

The M114 was a failure. The vehicle did not perform well in off-road conditions. It had trouble going up and down steep hills. The M114 was pulled out of U.S. Army service in 1975.

Chapter 3

A New Dune Buggy

The army looked for a new scout vehicle. They decided to test civilian dune buggies. Civilian means they are not used by the military.

In the early 1980s, the army bought 120 modified civilian dune buggies. Modified means they have been changed to improve their performance. They were called Fast Attack Vehicles (FAVs). They were given to the U.S. Army's 9th Infantry Division for testing.

The FAVs took part in many training exercises. FAVs were popular with the soldiers. They outperformed all other military vehicles.

The FAV was the first U.S. Army dune buggy.

THE PERSIAN GULF AREA

But the army decided not to buy any more FAVs. The army did not think the FAVs would survive on a battlefield. The FAVs had no armor to protect them from bullets and bombs.

Military Dune Buggies Come Back

A new military dune buggy appeared in 1991. It was called the Light Strike Vehicle (LSV). It was heavily used during the Persian Gulf War. This 1991 war was fought by the United States and other United Nations countries, including Great Britain, Egypt (EE-jipt), France, and Saudi Arabia (SOW-dee uh-RAY-be-uh). They fought against Iraq (eye-RACK), which had invaded Kuwait (koo-WAIT). The Persian Gulf War is also known as Operation Desert Storm.

The LSVs used in the Persian Gulf War were a military version of a dune buggy. These LSVs were built in the United States by the Chenowth Military Products company. The company is a well-known builder of civilian dune buggies.

LSVs are still used by the U.S. Army, the U.S. Navy, and the U.S. Marine Corps (KOHR). Several other countries have also bought LSVs. These dune buggies have been used for many different jobs. They have been used to do everything from catching drug smugglers to guarding nuclear power plants.

Persian Gulf War

U.S. Navy LSVs were the first vehicles to invade Iraq and Kuwait. They operated deep behind Iraqi lines for up to four days. Navy LSV crews reported the location of enemy targets. This information was passed along to U.S. pilots, who then destroyed the enemy targets with bombs.

LSV crews found Iraqi missile sites, radar stations, and command posts. LSV crews cut Iraqi communication lines when they found them. LSVs also conducted search-and-rescue missions for pilots who had been shot down.

Marine LSVs led the attack on Kuwait City. None of the U.S. Navy or U.S. Marine Corps LSVs suffered any losses during the Persian Gulf War.

Iraqi Scout Vehicles

The Iraqi army had no military dune buggies. They had to use very old Russian armored cars.

The U.S. Navy and U.S. Marine Corps used LSVs during the Persian Gulf War.

Russia

Russia is the largest country in the world. It covers more than one-tenth of the earth's entire land area. Russia stretches across the continents of Europe and Asia.

Russia was part of the Union of Soviet Socialist Republics (USSR) from 1922 to 1991. Russia was largest of the republics, and for the most part has taken the place of the USSR in world politics and in the world economy.

These armored cars were called BRDM-2s.

The BRDM-2 has a crew of four. The crew sits in the front. A gasoline engine is in the rear. The BRDM-2's top speed is 50 miles (80 kilometers) per hour. It can travel 310 miles (496 kilometers) on a full load of fuel.

The Iraqi army used an old Russian armored car called the BRDM-2.

Unlike the LSV, the BRDM-2 has some armor. But the armor can stop only small bullets. The BRDM-2 is armed with a large machine gun. The crew can also fire their own weapons from inside the vehicle. The BRDM-2s were no match for the quicker LSVs.

Chapter 4

The Light Strike Vehicle

Power for the LSV comes from a modified Volkswagen engine. The engine is air-cooled. It burns gasoline. It is located at the rear of the vehicle.

The LSV accelerates quickly. It can cross almost any type of ground. Its maximum speed is more than 85 miles (136 kilometers) per hour on a paved road.

LSVs are equipped with a 22-gallon (84-liter) fuel tank. They can travel more than 300 miles (480 kilometers) on a full tank of gas.

LSVs work well on almost any kind of terrain.

LSVs can operate a long time with very little maintenance.

With an extra fuel tank, the LSV can travel
more than 600 miles (960 kilometers).

LSVs have powerful disc brakes on all four
wheels. These brakes stop an LSV in a few
yards or meters. Scout vehicles need to stop
quickly if they are shot at by an enemy.

Design Features of the LSV

The LSV frame is made of high-strength steel tubing. A frame is a vehicle's skeleton. The engine and all other parts are attached to the frame.

The LSV frame is made from the same high-strength tubing used to build mountain bikes. Frame strength is important. The frame protects the crew if the LSV rolls over.

The LSV can be maintained with simple tools. This is an important feature for scout vehicles. If an LSV breaks down behind enemy lines, the crew could be captured or killed.

Low Maintenance

The LSV can operate longer in combat than other scout vehicles. Scout helicopters need more than 10 hours of maintenance for every hour of flying. Scout planes also need a lot of maintenance.

The LSV has an advanced suspension system. The suspension system is what makes a vehicle ride smoothly. It took 25 years of dune

buggy racing for Chenowth to develop the LSV's suspension system. It allows the LSV to cross rough ground at high speeds without shaking the crew too much.

Crew Features

The LSV crew sits in special bucket seats so they do not get tired on long missions. All crew members wear seat belts. These keep them in the vehicle when it travels over rough ground.

All LSV crew members wear helmets and goggles. The helmets have a built-in intercom system. The intercom is a radio system with microphones that let crew members talk to each other without shouting.

Improvements to the LSV

A new version of the LSV will be built soon. It will be known as the Advanced LSV. It will have a diesel engine instead of a gasoline engine. Diesel engines perform better at very low speeds and in cold weather.

In the future, the LSV may carry a small remote-control plane. The plane will be fitted with a miniature camera. The crew of an LSV will be able to launch the plane while they are hiding from the enemy.

The remote-control plane will be flown over enemy positions. The camera will send pictures back to the LSV crew. The LSV crew will then sneak away without being seen.

Chapter 5

LSV Weapons

The LSV was not designed to fight the enemy. The job of the LSV crew is to find the enemy. When they find the enemy, they are supposed to tell headquarters. Then the crew is supposed to leave.

Sometimes the LSV crew is discovered by the enemy. In case that happens, each LSV has one or two light machine guns called M60s. The M60 machine gun can fire up to 600 bullets per minute. The M60 bullets can hit a target more than 1,000 yards (910 meters) away.

This LSV has a rear-firing M60 machine gun.

Heavy Machine Gun

Most LSVs also carry a .50 caliber machine gun. Caliber is the size of the inside of the barrel measured in hundreths or thousandths of an inch. Caliber can also be measured in millimeters, in which case the number is always followed by the letters "mm."

The .50 caliber machine gun is an old weapon. It was first developed in 1919. It can fire up to 500 bullets per minute. It can shoot targets 2,500 yards (2,275 meters) away.

The .50 caliber machine gun fires a large bullet. It can be used to shoot down enemy helicopters. The .50 caliber bullet can also destroy light armored vehicles.

Grenade Launcher

Some LSVs carry a large automatic grenade launcher. The grenade launcher operates like a machine gun. It can fire 35 to 60 small grenades per minute. It works well against enemy soldiers in the open.

This LSV is fitted with a grenade launcher.

The grenade launcher can also fire an antitank grenade. Antitank means used to destroy tanks. This antitank grenade can blow a hole through two inches (five centimeters) of armor.

Many LSVs also carry antitank rocket launchers. Even though they are called antitank rockets, they are too small to destroy a tank. But they can destroy armored cars or troop carriers.

This Iraqi tank was hit and destroyed by a Hellfire missle fired from an LSV.

Other LSV Weapons

LSVs carry small antiaircraft missiles to protect the crew from enemy planes. Antiaircraft means used to shoot down planes and helicopters, protecting people and equipment on the ground.

The most common antiaircraft missile is the Stinger. The Stinger missile is attracted to the heat of aircraft engines. Once fired, it will fly into a plane's engine and then blow up.

LSVs can be fitted with the TOW antitank missile. TOW stands for Tubed Optically Wire-guided missile. The TOW missile is controlled by a small joystick. The joystick is like those used on video games. The gunner uses the joystick to aim and control the missile. The TOW missile can blow a hole in the thickest tank armor.

Hellfire Missile

The Hellfire antitank missile can also be fired from the LSV. The Hellfire is usually fired from a helicopter. It is aimed by pointing a laser beam at the target. A laser beam is an intense, narrow beam of light. The missile follows the laser beam to the target and destroys it.

In tests between tanks and LSVs, the tanks lost. The LSVs hit three tanks for every LSV hit. The LSVs were quick and agile during the tests. The tanks could not turn their cannons fast enough to shoot at the LSVs.

Machine Guns

Fiberglass Body

US ARMY

US ARMY

Off-Road Tire

Military Dune Buggy

Roll Bars

Radio Antenna

Bucket Seats

Off-Road Tire

Chapter 6

Safety Features

The LSV can be fitted with armor panels for protection. But the extra weight makes it slower. The crews of LSVs do not rely on armor. They are taught not to be seen. If they are not seen by the enemy, they will not be shot.

LSVs cannot be seen or heard very easily. They are small. They are painted in a camouflage (KAM-uh-flahj) pattern. LSVs have special low-noise mufflers.

Six LSVs can fit in this medium-duty helicopter.

Global Positioning System

Often, LSVs have to go into places without good maps. For an LSV crew, knowing where they are can be a matter of life and death. They must also know where the enemy is.

That is why many LSVs carry a global positioning system (GPS). The GPS is a small battery-powered device. It is better than a map or a compass.

The GPS uses signals from satellites in orbit around the earth. The satellites tell the LSV crews exactly where they are. The GPS can pinpoint a position anywhere in the world.

The Future of Military Dune Buggies

The LSV has proved itself in combat. It has performed missions where other military vehicles have failed. This has made the LSV an important part of the U.S. military. Many more LSVs will be used in the future.

This LSV is armed with a .50 caliber machine gun.

Words to Know

antiaircraft (AN-ti AIR-kraft)—weapons used to shoot down planes and helicopters

antitank (AN-ti TANGK)—weapons made especially to destroy tanks

armor (AR-mur)—anything used to protect vehicles, people, and cargo during combat

camouflage (KAM-uh-flahj)—any pattern that blends in with the surroundings

civilian (si-VIL-yuhn)—not intended for use by the military

dune buggy (DOON BUHG-ee)—small, fast vehicles powered by air-cooled Volkswagen engines, made for off-road racing

Global Positioning System (GLOHB-uhl puh-ZISH-uhn-ing SISS-tuhm)—a small battery-powered device that uses satellite signals to pinpoint a position anywhere in the world

Hellfire missile (HEL-fire MISS-uhl)—an antitank missile that follows a laser beam to a target

Persian Gulf War (PER-zjun GULF WOR)—
war fought by the United States and other
United Nations countries against Iraq in 1991;
also known as Operation Desert Storm.

scout (SKOUT)—person who spies on enemy
troops

scout vehicle (SKOUT VEE-uh-kuhl)—the
machines scouts drive while they are spying on
the enemy

Stinger (STING-ur)—antiaircraft missiles that
protect people and vehicles on the land against
attacks from helicopters and airplanes

tank (TANGK)—enclosed vehicles protected
with heavy armor

TOW (TOH)—an antitank missile that is
controlled by a small joystick

tracks (TRAKS)—metal belts that run around
wheels on both sides of a vehicle

To Learn More

Chant, Christopher. *The Marshall Cavendish Illustrated Guide to Military Vehicles*. New York: Marshall Cavendish, 1989.

Crismon, Fred W. *U.S. Military Wheeled Vehicles*. Sarasota, Fla: Crestline Publications, 1983.

Foss, Christopher F. *Military Vehicles of the World*. New York: Charles Scribner's Sons, 1976.

Hoggs, Ivan V. and John Weeks. *The Illustrated Encyclopedia of Military Vehicles*. London: New Burlington Books, 1980.

Useful Addresses

History and Museum Division
Headquarters U.S. Marine Corps
Washington, DC 20380

Marine Corps Joint Public Affairs Office
Marine Corps Base
Camp Pendleton, CA 92055

U.S. Army Transportation Museum
Building 300 (Besson Hall)
Fort Eustic, VA 23604-5260

U.S. Navy Public Affairs Office
1200 Navy Pentagon
Room 2E341
Washington, DC 20350-1200

Internet Sites

Dune Buggy
http://www.nosc.mil/robots/land/dbuggy/
dbuggy.html

The 4x4 Web Page
http://www.off-road.com

Operation Desert Storm
http://www.geocities.com/Athens/65061

WWII—Another Look
http://amug.org/~avishai/WWIp2.html

The FAV was not sucessful because it did not offer
protection from enemy fire.

Index